Maps and Symbols

Susan Lomas

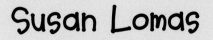

WAYLAND

Geography First

Titles in this series
Coasts • Islands • Maps and Symbols
Mountains • Rivers • Volcanoes

© 2004 White-Thomson Publishing Ltd

Produced for Hodder Wayland by
White-Thomson Publishing Ltd
2/3 St Andrew's Place
Lewes, East Sussex
BN7 1UP

Geography consultant: John Lace, School Adviser
Editor: Katie Orchard
Picture research: Glass Onion Pictures
Designer: Chris Halls at Mind's Eye Design Ltd, Lewes
Artist: Peter Bull

Published in Great Britain in 2004 by Hodder Wayland,
an imprint of Hodder Children's Books.

This paperback edition published in 2006 by Wayland,
an imprint of Hachette Children's Books.

The right of Susan Lomas to be identified as the
author has been asserted by her in accordance with
the Copyright, Designs and Patents Act 1988.

British Library Cataloguing in Publication Data
Lomas, Susan
  Maps and Symbols. - (Geography First)
  1. Cartography - Juvenile literature 2. Map reading -
  Juvenile literature
  I. Title II. Orchard, Katie
  551.4'83

ISBN-10: 0 7502 4631 6
ISBN-13: 978 0 7502 4631 6

Printed in China

Wayland
An imprint of Hachette Children's Books
338 Euston Road, London NW1 3BH

Cover: A bird's-eye view of New York, USA.
Title page: These schoolchildren are studying a globe.
Contents page: An aerial photograph.
Futher information page: These schoolchildren have
found Africa on a map of the world.

Acknowledgements:
The author and publisher would like to thank the following for their permission to reproduce the
following photographs: Corbis *cover,* 5 (Layne Kennedy), 6 (Michal Heron), 10 (Michael S. Yamashita),
12 (Onne van der Wal), 13 (David Samuel Robbins), 17 (Ed Bock), 22 (Stocktreck); Ecoscene 14 (Peter Hulme),
24 (Mike Whittle), 26 (Alex Bartel); Angela Hampton 11; Hodder Wayland Picture Library *title page,*
chapter openers, 8 (Geonex), 28, 31; Popperfoto 20 (Bobby Yip/Reuters), 23 (Toshiyuki Aizawa/Reuters), 25;
Science Photo Library 7 (Frank Zullo).

Words in bold **like this** are explained in the glossary on page 30.

Contents

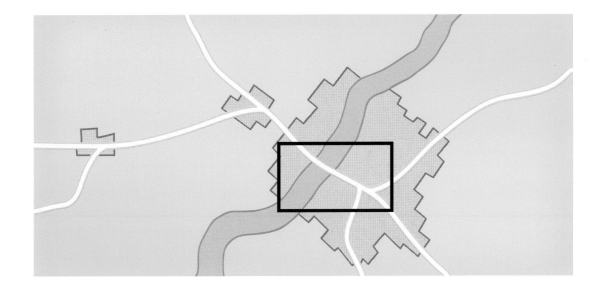

What is a map?

A map is a flat drawing of a real place. It shows the shape and size of the place and where things are. A map can give a lot more information about a place than a photograph can.

Some maps show a small area, such as a room or a park. Other maps show larger areas, such as whole countries, continents or even the world.

Mapping the World

North America

Europe

Asia

Africa

South America

Australasia

Antarctica

The Earth is really a sphere, like a ball, but a map is flat.

Maps of larger areas may give the names of countries and cities. They also show important features such as rivers and hills.

Different types of map

People can use maps to help them find their way around or to help them in their work. Town planners use maps to decide where to put buildings. Some people use maps for hobbies such as hill walking.

▼ *This **architect** is looking at a map of a building site. The map shows where new buildings will go.*

There are many different types of map. Sailors use special maps of the sea to travel across oceans and enter **ports**. Maps can also be used to show things such as the weather or the stars.

▼ Astronomers use powerful telescopes to see far into space. Star maps help them identify what they see.

A bird's-eye view

A good way to show exactly where things are is to picture how they look from above. This view is called a **bird's-eye view** because it shows what a bird might see if it was looking down from the sky.

▼ *Things that you are used to seeing from the side can look very different from above. This photograph was taken from an aeroplane.*

Many maps show a bird's-eye view of an area. These maps make it easy to see how far apart different features are and how much space they take up. Maps that show small areas such as a classroom or a house in this way are called **plans**.

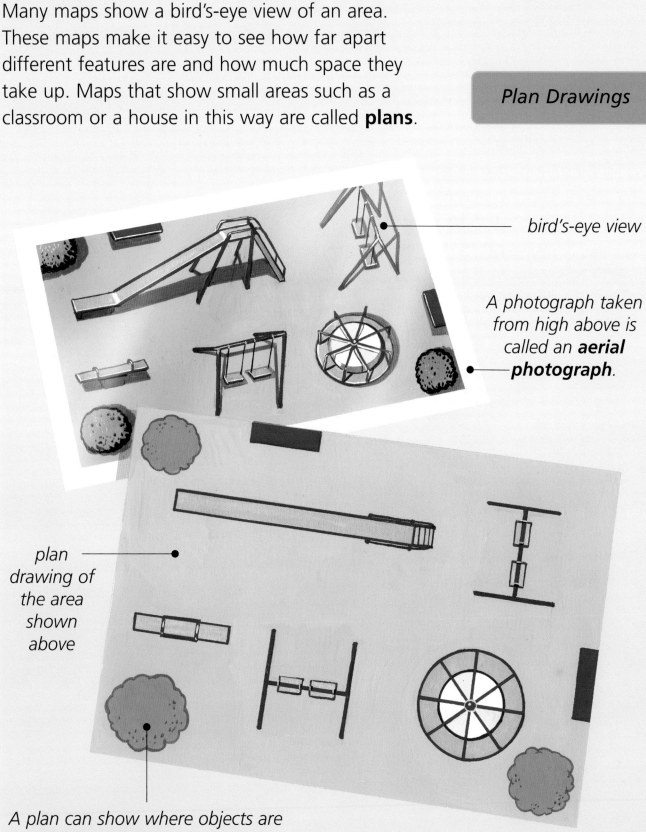

bird's-eye view

A photograph taken from high above is called an **aerial photograph**.

plan drawing of the area shown above

A plan can show where objects are and how far apart they are.

Mapping landmarks

People may use maps of larger areas, such as villages or towns, to help them find their way from one building to another.

▼ *This is a bird's-eye view of New York, USA. There are so many buildings that a visitor would need a map to find their way around.*

If someone asks you for directions to go to a place, you may use **landmarks** to help them. You might use phrases like, 'go straight past the shop', 'turn right at the school', or 'pass the church on your left'.

▼ When asking for directions, it is helpful to find a landmark that you can see on the map. Then you know exactly where you are.

Maps put landmarks into a drawing that is easy to follow. They show exactly where each landmark is compared to everything else.

Direction

When people travel long distances, they use the words north, south, east and west to give directions instead of right, left or straight on. This is especially useful if there are no landmarks.

▼ *Ships may travel for long periods without seeing anything but water. They need to know which direction is north to find their way.*

Maps usually show north at the top and south at the bottom. People find the direction of north using a **compass**. A compass has a **magnetic** needle inside, which always points north.

By matching up the compass point with north on a map, travellers can always find out which direction they are heading in.

Grids on maps

At first glance, a map can look very confusing. It may seem like a jumble of lines, shapes and colours.

To make them easier to use, maps that show large areas of land are broken up into a pattern of vertical and horizontal lines, called a **grid**.

▼ Grids break up a large area into smaller pieces. This scientist is using a grid to study the number of plants found in a small area.

A grid divides a map into smaller sections. The sides of each grid section may be labelled with letters or numbers. These make it easier to find places or landmarks on a map and describe where they are.

Each row is labelled with a number.

Each column has a letter at the top.

Together, the numbers and letters show where a landmark is.

The church is in grid square D7.

The school is in grid square F4.

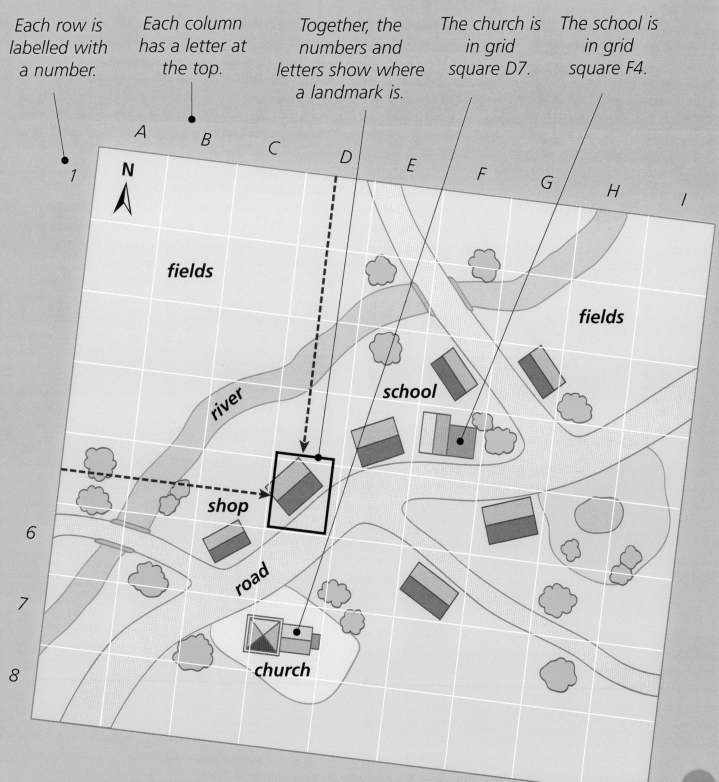

Dividing up the world

A **globe** is a small model of the Earth. A globe can be divided into smaller sections by a series of imaginary circles, called **latitude** and **longitude**.

Lines of longitude pass through the **North Pole** and **South Pole**. Lines of latitude circle the Earth at right angles to longitude lines. The **Equator** is the longest line of latitude.

The Globe

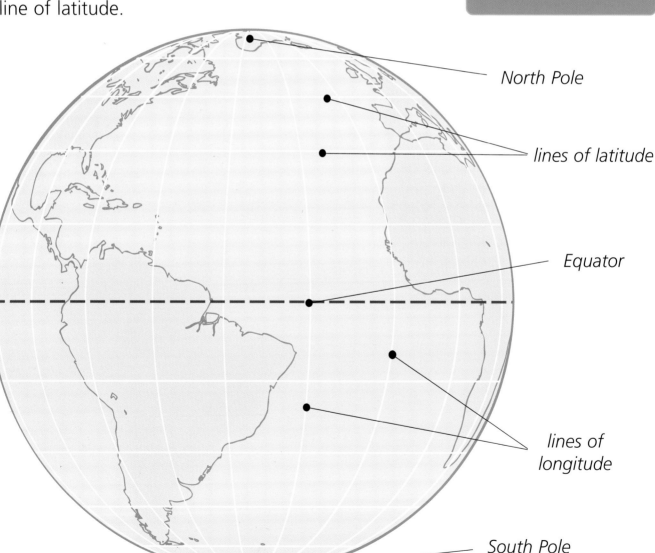

North Pole

lines of latitude

Equator

lines of longitude

South Pole

On a flat map of the world, lines of longitude and latitude look like a grid. Lines of longitude go from top to bottom and lines of latitude go from left to right.

▼ You can see the lines of longitude and latitude on this map.

Height of the land

Maps are flat, but the land is not. Some areas of countryside have hills, mountains, valleys or cliffs. Some maps need to show the height of the land on a flat piece of paper. This is done in several ways.

Mapping Land Height

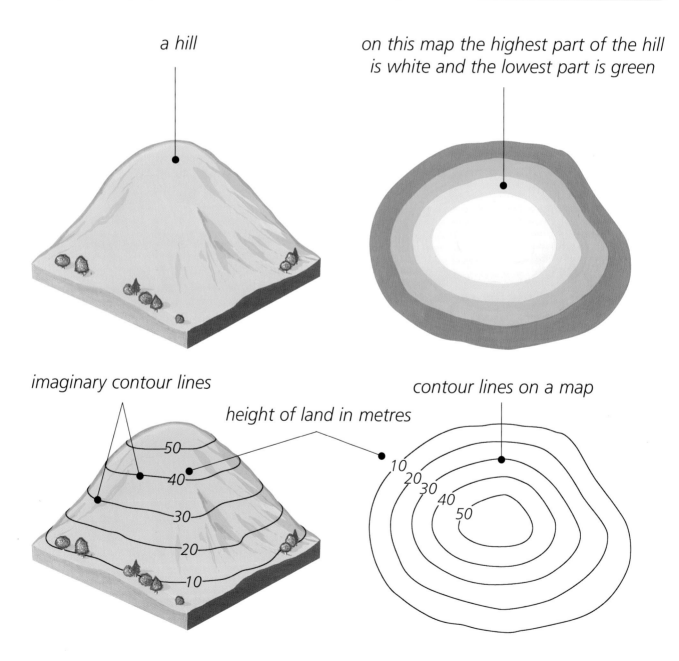

a hill

on this map the highest part of the hill is white and the lowest part is green

imaginary contour lines

height of land in metres

contour lines on a map

50
40
30
20
10

10
20
30
40
50

Height on a map is sometimes shown with colours, such as white or purple for high ground and green for lower ground.

Other maps show the height of land using **contours**. Contours are lines that connect places of the same height.

▼ *To show steep land, like the hills in this photograph, contour lines on a map appear close together. The flat areas have no contours at all.*

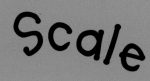

Scale

A map shows a large area of land on a small piece of paper. Before a mapmaker draws a map, the large area is carefully measured, or **surveyed**. All the measurements are reduced by the same amount, so they are small enough to fit on the paper. This is called a **scale** drawing.

▼ *This is a **scale model** of a dam that is being built in the Three Gorges area of China. The real thing will be many, many times bigger.*

The **scale bar** of a map shows how much smaller than real life a map is. Small-scale maps show large areas with very little detail. A map of the world, for example, is a very small-scale map.

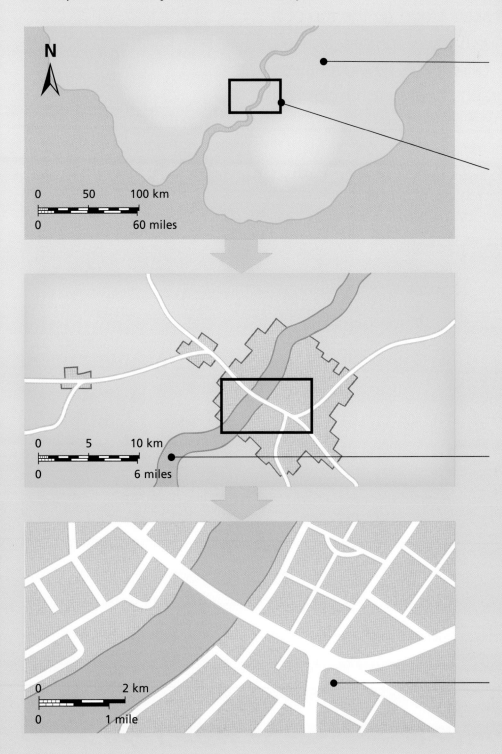

This small-scale map shows a large area of land. There is not very much detail.

This rectangle shows the area that the map below focuses on.

A scale bar is shown in the bottom left-hand corner of each map. As the scale of a map gets bigger, more detail is shown.

This is the largest-scale map of the area. There is much more detail.

Making maps

Many years ago, mapmakers stood on the top of a high point such as a church tower to draw a map of the area around them. Later, pilots flew over areas and took aerial photographs from which maps could be drawn.

▼ Satellites like this one take detailed photographs of the world from space.

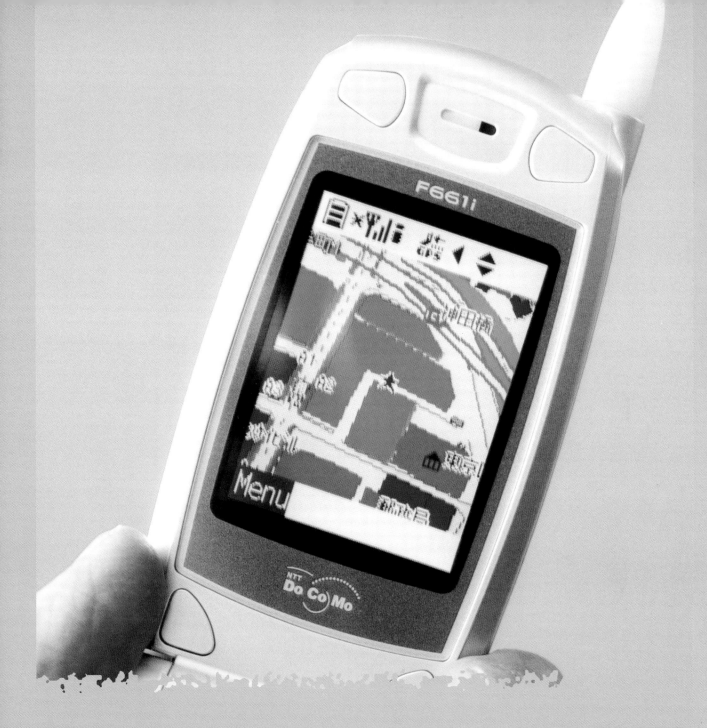

Mapmaking has come a long way since then. Today, maps are produced by computers, using **satellite images** taken from space.

The Earth's landscape is forever changing. New airports, roads and towns are being built all the time. People will always need new maps to help them find their way.

▲ *Mobile phones like this one can now show a person where they are, using information from satellites.*

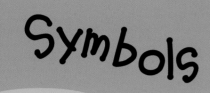

Symbols

Not everything can be shown on maps, especially small-scale ones. There is simply not enough room to draw pictures of everything on a map.

▼ These symbols warn motorists in Australia that several different types of animal might cross this road.

BOBTAILS

CROSSING

Mapmakers use simple signs, called **symbols**, to show as much information as possible and to make the map easier to read.

Symbols are often simple drawings that show what things are and where they are. They are used on maps to show the position of important landmarks, such as woods, rivers and roads.

▲ **In-car navigation systems** are electronic maps for cars. They have lots of symbols on them, showing roads, parks and traffic lights.

Symbols on maps

Mapmakers have to decide which landmarks to include on a map. A large-scale map needs to show lots of detail, and may have lots of symbols.

▼ *A map of this part of London would need to have symbols for important buildings, a river, bridges and green areas.*

Some symbols are a special shape, for example, a tree shape might be used to show a forest. Other symbols use colour. Different sizes or types of road may be shown on a map in different colours.

All the symbols and colours used on a map are explained in a **key** so that everyone can understand what they mean.

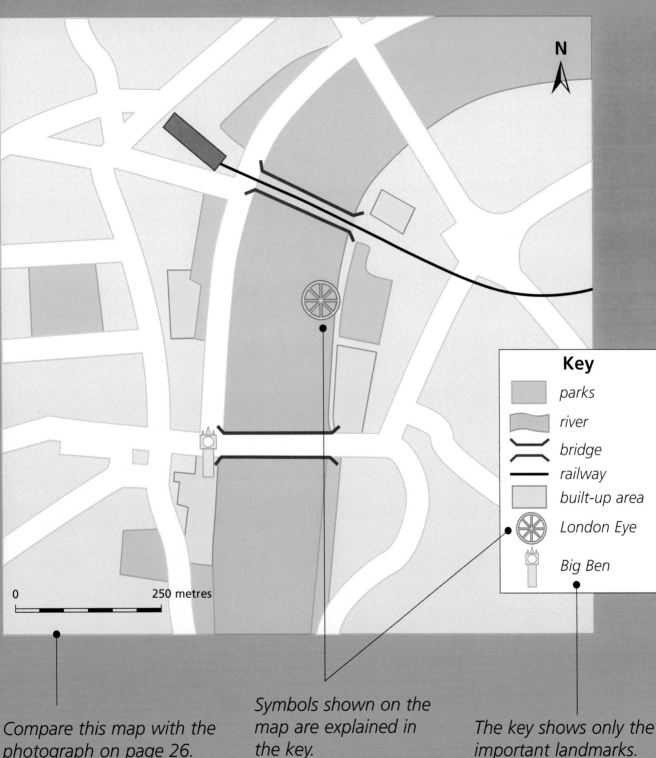

Key

parks

river

bridge

railway

built-up area

London Eye

Big Ben

0   250 metres

Compare this map with the photograph on page 26.

Symbols shown on the map are explained in the key.

The key shows only the important landmarks.

Make your own map

You could draw your own map or plan. You might want to start by drawing a plan of somewhere you know well, such as a room in your house.

You will need: a tape measure, a ruler, some paper, an eraser, a pencil, coloured pencils and a compass.

1. Measure each side of the room.

2. Choose a scale so that you can draw the outline of the room on the piece of paper. Perhaps a scale of 1 metre to 10 centimetres would work well. Show the scale of your map at the bottom.

3. When you have drawn the outline, measure things like the windows, your bed and any other furniture in your room. Then measure how far along the wall each item is. Put them in the correct place on your plan.

4. Draw some symbols to represent some of the things in your bedroom, for example toys or a lamp. Use colour if you want to.

5. Make a key to tell you what these symbols mean.

6. If you have a compass, try to show which way is north on your plan.

7. Add a grid on to your plan. Don't forget to put numbers up the side and letters across the bottom.

8. Colour in your map.

You could give the map to a friend and ask them to find objects in your room.

▲ If this girl drew a plan of her bedroom, it might look like the one on page 29.

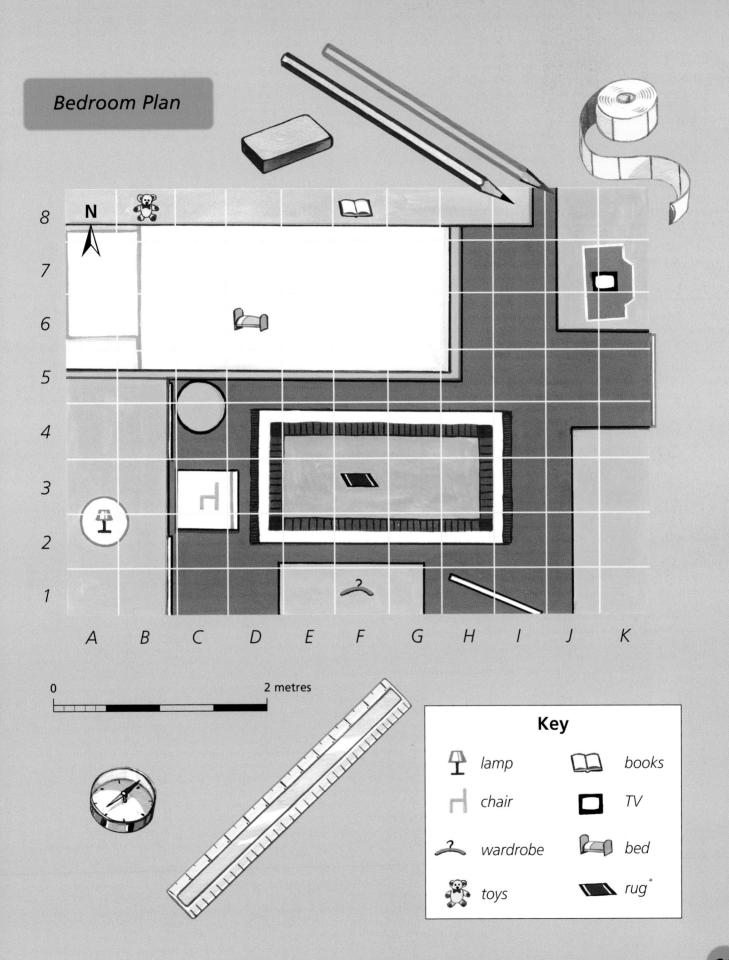

Bedroom Plan

Key

- lamp
- chair
- wardrobe
- toys
- books
- TV
- bed
- rug

Glossary

Aerial photographs Photographs taken from above the ground, such as from an aeroplane.

Architect A person who designs and plans buildings.

Bird's-eye view A view of an area from above, such as an aerial photograph.

Compass An instrument used for finding direction.

Contour A line that joins points of the same height above sea level.

Equator An imaginary line around the middle of the Earth.

Globe A ball-shaped model of the Earth.

Grid A series of lines drawn on a map from top to bottom and from left to right.

In-car navigation system A computer in a car that shows where the car is on a map, by receiving satellite signals.

Key This explains what symbols on a map mean.

Landmarks Important features of a place, such as roads, forests or buildings.

Latitude Imaginary lines running from east to west around the globe.

Longitude Imaginary lines that run at right angles to the Equator and meet at the North and South Poles.

Magnetic The Earth acts as if it had a giant bar magnet inside it. The points on the Earth's surface just over the two opposite ends of the 'magnet' are called the magnetic North and South Poles.

North Pole The point on the globe that is furthest north.

Plan A map of a small area, such as a room or a building.

Port A safe place for ships to moor.

Satellite images Photographs taken from space.

Scale A way of showing the size of a map compared to real life. For example, on a 1:100 map, 1 centimetre on the map represents 100 centimetres on the ground.

Scale bar A measuring rule on a map that shows how far apart places are in real life.

Scale model A smaller than life-sized model of an object.

South Pole The point on the globe that is furthest south.

Survey To measure distances and angles to work out the size and shape of an area accurately.

Symbol A small picture or shape that gives information on a map.

Further information

Books to Read:

Basic Mapwork Skills by Simon Ross and David Jones (Nelson Thornes, 2003)

Children's Activity Atlas by Neil Morris (Belitha Press, 1998)

Maps and Globes (Step-by-Step Geography) by Sabrina Crewe (Franklin Watts, 2002)

Maps and Journeys (Roundabouts) by Kate Petty and Jakki Wood (A&C Black, 2000)

Maps and Symbols (Geography Starts Here!) by Angela Royston (Hodder Wayland, 2001)

Pam's Maps (Flying Foxes) by Pippa Goodheart (Heinemann Library, 2003)

Index

All the numbers in **bold** refer to photographs and illustrations as well as text.